SEP 1 1 2015

ELK GROVE VILLAGE PUBLIC LIBRARY

3 1250 01115 5482

P9-CMV-210

Discarded By Elk Grove
Village Public Library

ELK GROVE VILLAGE PUBLIC LIBRARY
1001 WELLINGTON AVE
ELK GROVE VILLAGE, IL 60007
(847) 439-0447

SURVIVAL CHALLENGE

COLD!

Could YOU stay warm in the world's wildest places?

STEPHANIE TURNBULL

A⁺

Smart Apple Media

Published by Smart Apple Media,
an imprint of Black Rabbit Books
P.O. Box 3263, Mankato, Minnesota, 56002
www.blackrabbitbooks.com

U.S. publication copyright © 2015 Smart Apple Media.
International copyright reserved in all countries.
No part of this book may be reproduced in any form
without written permission from the publisher.

Designed and illustrated by Guy Callaby
Edited by Mary-Jane Wilkins

Cataloging-in-Publication Data is available from the Library of Congress

ISBN 978-1-62588-213-4

Photo acknowledgements
t = top; c = center; b = bottom; r = right; l = left
folio image iStockphoto/Thinkstock; page 2t Evikka, b TerraceStudio/both
Shutterstock; 3 Stephen Finn/Shutterstock; 4t cappi thompson/Shutterstock;
4-5 Tyler Olson/Shutterstock; 5r DJTaylor/Shutterstock; 6t Arcady, b Galyna
Andrushko/both Shutterstock; 7 Pavel L Photo and Video/Shutterstock;
8t Lack-O'Keen, l Arch. Giacomo Longo, r Nickolay Stanev/all Shutterstock;
9 Photoexpert/Shutterstock; 11t LianeM, b Varygin/both Shutterstock;
12 maga, 13 Ainars Aunins/both Shutterstock; 14t Andrew Scheck,
c marekuliasz/both Shutterstock; 15 tanikewak/Shutterstock; 18 Tom Grundy/
Shutterstock; 19 CandyBox Images/Shutterstock; 20 iStockphoto/Thinkstock;
21 Friday Ivo/Shutterstock; 23 Nejron Photo/Shutterstock
Cover t iStock/Thinkstock, b Florin Stana/Shutterstock

Printed in China

DAD0056
032014
9 8 7 6 5 4 3 2 1

CONTENTS

TAKE THE CHALLENGE 4

KNOW THE DANGERS 6

ACT FAST 8

LIGHT A STOVE 10

MAKE A FIRE 12

LIGHT YOUR FIRE 14

TRY OTHER METHODS 16

THINK SMART 18

PUT IT OUT 20

GLOSSARY AND WEB SITES 22

INDEX 24

TAKE THE CHALLENGE

Imagine you're an intrepid explorer battling through a howling storm in the wilderness.

Swirling sleet and snow whip your face and drench you to the bone, while the bitter wind numbs your entire body.

You stumble to a halt, exhausted and shivering uncontrollably. The horrible truth sinks in: you're too cold to keep going. If you don't act quickly, you could die.

Your challenge is to warm up —fast. Can you do it?

Sudden, heavy rain can soak you in seconds, making your body temperature (and your spirits) plummet.

5

KNOW THE DANGERS

You're in a serious situation. Being out in extremely low temperatures doesn't mean cold feet and a runny nose—it means lost toes and complete body breakdown! Spotting the danger signs quickly could save your life.

⬆ *Be sensible and check whether to expect low temperatures before setting off.*

Energetic hiking may keep you warm during the day, but remember that it will be colder at night.

EXTREME COLD

When your body is exposed to very cold, wet or windy weather, it loses heat about 20 times faster than normal. Having a dangerously low body temperature is called **hypothermia**.

HYPOTHERMIA CHECKLIST

Do you have any symptoms of hypothermia? Here are some:

* Violent shivering
* Tiredness
* Slurred speech
* Confusion
* Slow, shallow breathing
* Difficulty moving

FROSTBITE

Another danger is **frostbite**, when parts of your body most exposed to the cold, such as hands and feet, start to throb and ache. Eventually the skin becomes hard and waxy. Body parts that are badly damaged by frostbite may never recover.

◐ *These are the danger points for frostbite: nose, ears, fingers and toes.*

Hunting guides Jim Bailey and Jesse Gray were in a tiny aircraft in thick fog and snow over Alaska when they crashed in the icy Bering Sea. Numb with cold and shock, they swam ashore, but hypothermia soon set in. They stumbled along the snowy shore for two days, exhausted. At last an aircraft picked them up. They were lucky to be alive.

REAL LIFE SURVIVAL

ACT FAST

What do you do to avoid hypothermia and frostbite, or treat symptoms if you're affected? Don't panic. Read on—then act FAST.

FIND SHELTER

Don't keep trudging on in the hope of reaching camp—you need to find shelter now. Anywhere will do —an overhanging rock, a cave, a hollow tree or even a large pile of logs or leaves that you could crawl behind or underneath.

Remember that animals use natural shelters too, so check yours is empty before settling in!

REAL LIFE SURVIVAL

Alexander Zverev was canoeing in China in 2007 when his boat capsized in the remote Yurungkax River. Trembling with cold, he stumbled to shore and found shelter in a cave. He made a bed of tree branches and stayed there—chilly, but safe—until he was found, 20 days later.

USE SUPPLIES

Take off any wet clothes and pile on spare layers from your backpack. If you have a sleeping bag, climb inside it. If you're smart you'll also be carrying energy-rich snacks and a thermos with a hot drink. These should help you feel better.

⮕ *Move away from the entrance, if possible, to avoid cold winds.*

⮐ *Good backpacks can hold a surprising amount of useful survival kit.*

TREAT FROSTBITE

Frostbitten skin needs warming gently, so wrap affected areas in blankets or spare clothes. DON'T be tempted to rub or massage the skin or you'll damage it. As skin warms, it will feel painful. You'll need medical help as soon as you can get it.

LIGHT A STOVE

You're out of the howling wind and driving snow. But the light is fading and the prospect of shivering all night on the damp ground is bleak. Only one thing will help—fire.

CHECK YOUR KIT

Let's assume you packed a decent survival kit before heading out into such remote territory. This should contain essentials such as food, drink, bedding, clothing, a compass, map and first aid supplies. You may also have a small cooking **stove**.

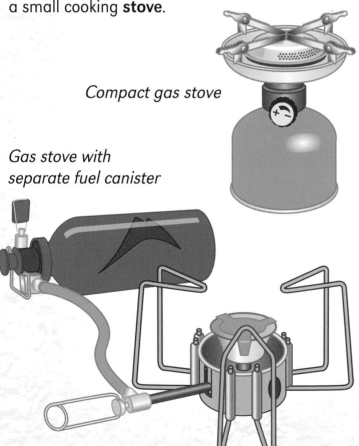

Compact gas stove

Gas stove with separate fuel canister

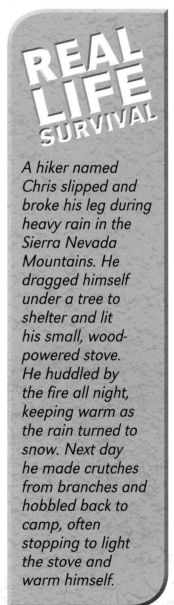

REAL LIFE SURVIVAL

A hiker named Chris slipped and broke his leg during heavy rain in the Sierra Nevada Mountains. He dragged himself under a tree to shelter and lit his small, wood-powered stove. He huddled by the fire all night, keeping warm as the rain turned to snow. Next day he made crutches from branches and hobbled back to camp, often stopping to light the stove and warm himself.

KEEP IT LIT

Camping stoves don't give out much heat, but every little helps. Place the stove on a flat surface and light it carefully. Shield it from drafts so it doesn't blow out.

⮕ *Using your stove to heat a tin of soup will make you feel so much better.*

STAY SAFE

Don't use your stove in a completely enclosed space such as a small cave, as it will give off dangerous **carbon monoxide**. And don't put it too close to branches or other material that could catch fire if it suddenly flared up.

MAKE A FIRE

You can make a fire if you don't have a camping stove. This will keep you warm, give you light, protect you from animals and may even help a rescue party spot you. But it can also be very dangerous. So pay attention!

CHOOSE A SPOT

Find a clear, open area. Brush away leaves and twigs so your fire won't spread. Make sure there are no overhanging branches, or the whole area may go up in flames.

If you can, dig a shallow trench for your fire to shield it from wind.

FIND FUEL

Now you need something to burn.

1. *Make a pile of soft, fluffy or fine material that will catch fire easily. Shredded paper, moss or crumbly, rotten wood all work well. This is called tinder.*

◔ *The dry, spongy inner layer of fungus makes good tinder.*

2. *Prop small twigs and sticks loosely around your tinder pile. This is called kindling and will produce flames and heat to get the fire going.*

3. *Finally, find larger pieces of wood to use later to keep your fire burning. Dry, dead branches burn well.*

In 1887, an explorer named Francis Younghusband made a perilous journey across the Himalayan Mountains. One night Francis and his guides had no wood for fuel, but they managed to light handfuls of grass in a dry, sheltered spot. It was a small fire, but it kept them alive through the long, cold night.

REAL LIFE SURVIVAL

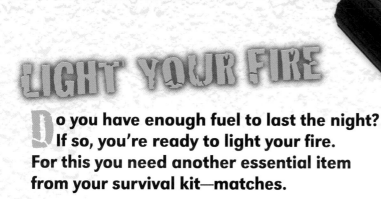

LIGHT YOUR FIRE

Do you have enough fuel to last the night? If so, you're ready to light your fire. For this you need another essential item from your survival kit—matches.

↺ *High marks if you brought waterproof matches like these!*

DRY MATCHES

Ordinary matches must be kept in a sealed container. If they're wet, they won't strike. You can also dip them in melted wax, which forms a waterproof coating as it cools.

LIGHTING TIPS

Strike a match near the tinder. Be careful not to burn your fingers, and don't throw the match away until you're sure it's out. Matches burn up quickly, so try lighting a long paper or bark **taper** to make the flame last longer.

FEED THE FIRE

Once the tinder is burning, flames and heat will rise and light the kindling. Start adding bigger pieces of wood to keep it going. Don't put on too much at once or you'll cut off the **oxygen** supply.

🎧 *Keep an eye on your fire. Don't make it too big or you'll waste fuel—but don't let it go out, either.*

John Murphy was hiking in Oregon when disaster struck—he fell and injured his knee. There was no way he could get back to camp before night, but fortunately he was carrying good fire-lighting equipment. He used his phone to call for help and stayed warm by his fire until rescuers arrived.

REAL LIFE SURVIVAL

TRY OTHER METHODS

Lost your matches? Try a different way of making fire—but be warned, it may take a lot of time and skill. Can you do it?

STEEL AND FLINT

An emergency steel and **flint** kit is good to have with you. These handy hiking sets contain a curved piece of steel and a sharp flint that you can use to make sparks.

Steel

1. *Hold the steel over the tinder. Strike the flint against the steel in a downward motion. Sparks should fly down toward the tinder.*

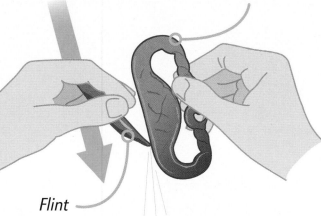

Flint

2. *When a spark falls on the tinder and a glowing red **ember** appears, blow on it steadily to help it catch fire. It may help to hold the tinder to give it more air. Put it down carefully when it starts to burn.*

FRICTION STICKS

In the past, people such as Native Americans used **friction** sticks to make fire. You need a smooth, straight stick, a flat piece of wood and a knife.

1. Using your knife, dig out a hollow in the wood, big enough for the stick to fit in. Carve a notch from the hole to the edge of the wood.

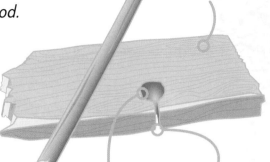

Friction stick

Wood

Hollow   Notch

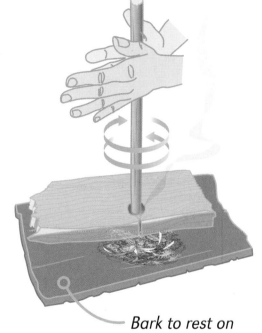

Bark to rest on

2. Stand the wood on some tinder and spin the stick very quickly in the hollow. As the two pieces of wood rub together, they make heat, which should eventually produce an ember. This should fall through the notch and onto your tinder. Good luck!

Charles Horton fell and broke his leg while skiing in Colorado. He had a few matches so he used them to light some branches and stay warm through the night. But with no matches left, the next night was cold and miserable—and so were the next six before he was rescued. If only he'd taken more matches, or a steel and flint kit!

REAL LIFE SURVIVAL

THINK SMART

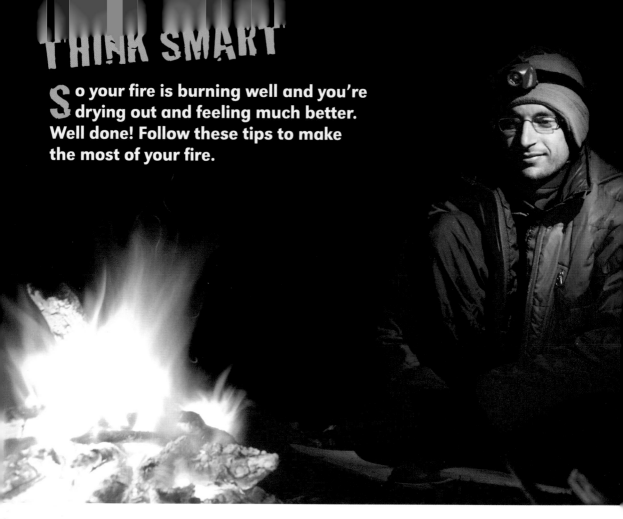

So your fire is burning well and you're drying out and feeling much better. Well done! Follow these tips to make the most of your fire.

MAKE A STAR

If you're short of wood, place six or eight large branches around the fire in a star shape. As the ends burn down, move the branches inward. It won't be as warm or bright as a normal fire, but it will last longer and use less fuel.

USE THE HEAT

If you're still cold, make your fire more efficient by piling up a wall of logs or rocks near the fire. This will reflect heat back toward you and keep your whole body warmer.

CLEVER COOKING

Feeling hungry? Hang a cooking pot over your fire using one branch propped firmly against another, or rest a pan on two logs placed on either side of the fire.

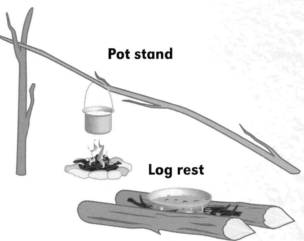

Pot stand

Log rest

⟳ *Remember that cooking pots will get very hot, so don't burn your hands.*

An archaeologist named Chris Kavanaugh was stranded with his team on an island off the coast of California. Some of the men started hacking at branches to make a fire, but Chris went to the beach and gathered armfuls of driftwood. Soon he had made several roaring fires that kept everyone warm all night. He was smart enough to think ahead and save his energy.

REAL LIFE SURVIVAL

PUT IT OUT

Finally dawn breaks and you stretch your stiff legs next to the glowing embers of your fire. You made it through the night! But don't set off yet—put out that fire first.

Even the smallest camp fire can cause a terrible blaze if left to get out of control.

Peter Fleming was a writer who climbed a tree to watch a distant forest fire in Brazil. Fire raced across the land and the sky was full of burning embers that started new fires wherever they fell. Suddenly hot sparks burned him, so he leapt from the tree and ran downhill to a river bank. He'd learned that fire moves fast!

VANISHING ACT

Throwing handfuls of soil onto your fire is a good way of cutting off its oxygen supply and putting it out.

When it looks dead, rake over the embers with twigs to help them cool. Turn over any stones.

Pour cold water or pile snow on the embers. Check that no vegetation or roots nearby are hot or smoking. Fire can spread underground through smoldering tree roots!

TIDY UP

You survived your night in the wild, so show the environment some respect. Clear up the scar your fire made and try to leave the land as you found it. Put stones back where you found them and move any cleared vegetation back into its place.

↻ *Don't leave your fire site looking like this!*

21

carbon monoxide
A colorless, odorless, poisonous gas formed when certain fuels, such as natural gas, burn without enough oxygen.

ember
A glowing, hot fragment of wood or other natural fuel. Embers can start a fire and also remain when a fire has burned right down.

flint
A very hard, greyish-black stone that breaks into pieces with sharp edges. When you strike a piece of flint hard against steel, it creates sparks.

friction
The effect of rubbing one object or surface against another.

frostbite
A very painful condition in which skin and other body parts are damaged by extreme cold.

hypothermia
A condition in which the body's temperature drops dangerously low because of exposure to cold, wet or windy weather.

oxygen
A colorless, odorless gas in the air. We need oxygen to breathe and fires need it to burn.

stove
A piece of portable camping equipment that burns fuel such as gas, gasoline or paraffin.

taper
A thin strip of wood, paper or other material that is used to keep a flame burning.

www.wilderness-survival-skills.com/how-to-make-a-fire.html
Advice on materials to use for building a fire.

www.wildwoodsurvival.com
Unusual methods of making fire!

www.comingbackalive.com
Essential safety facts, including information about hypothermia and frostbite.

INDEX

backpack 9

camp 8, 10, 15
carbon monoxide 11, 22
caves 8, 9, 11
compass 10
cooking 19

embers 16, 17, 20, 21, 22

feet 6, 7
fingers 7
fire 10, 11, 12, 13, 14, 15, 16,
 17, 18, 19, 20, 21
first aid supplies 10
fog 7
food 9, 10
friction sticks 17
frostbite 7, 8, 9, 22
fuel 10, 13, 14, 15, 18

hands 7
hiking 6, 10, 15
hypothermia 7, 8, 22

kindling 13, 15

map 10
matches 14, 16, 17

oxygen 15, 21, 22

phone 15

rain 5, 10

shelter 8, 9, 10
shivering 5, 7, 10
skin 7, 9
sleeping bag 9
snow 4, 7, 10, 21
steel and flint 16, 17, 22
storms 4
stove 10, 11, 12, 22
survival kit 9, 10, 14

tapers 14, 22
tinder 13, 14, 15, 16, 17
toes 6, 7

wind 4, 7, 9, 10, 12
wood 10, 13, 15, 17, 18, 19